MOONLIGHT REFLECTIONS

Moonlight Reflections

Nicole Hernandez

From one lost star to another,
as small as we may feel,
we keep the night sky full and bright.
-Nicole Hernandez

Contents

1

When The Heart Yearns

<u>Would I?</u>

If I knew you back then,
Would I love you again
Or would I stay away
Would I let you back in
Just as I always did
Or would I be different
Would I lose all my strength
That I fought to regain
Would you take it away
If I tried to run free
Would you chase after me
Like a beast and its prey
Would I fail you again
Leaving me alone in bed
Just like you did back then
If I met you again
I know I'd hurt you instead
Just to see how it felt
Just as you did to me.

<u>What You Did To Me</u>

If I could go back in time,
I never would have kissed you
If I knew it'd lead to my endless tears on empty nights.
Four walls muffle broken sounds
Of painful cries and bladed screams,
Silent as my knees hit the ground
The last night you would leave me.
Blind, how I refuse to see
The sharp knife you ran through me,
I wonder if the pain will cease
As torture scars heal seemingly.
I swear my revenge by the moon
And bless it by the immortal sun,
I will drag you down to hell
And watch you burn eternally.

<u>My Ocean</u>

I was willing to risk it all for you,
To leave everything behind if it meant being with you
Content with being alone, if I'd be alone with you.
And that was all I needed

But at the end of the day
I was alone, completely alone
And you were nowhere to be seen
You were just a wave that came close to shore
but left as soon as you appeared
Only leaving hints of yourself behind
Even after you promised to stay time and time again

You left me stranded at sea
Knowing I can't swim
destined to drown in your absence

You stood by as I tore myself apart for you
You watched as I defended you
Yet still deemed me unfaithful
You destroyed me just as a tsunami destroys a city
Still I wonder how I survived that god awful wreckage

<u>My Sickness</u>

No matter how many times I tell people I've moved on
The scars you left on my wrist still burn
Just as haunting as the ghost of your touch

My gut twists in agony remembering how I trusted you
And I cry recalling how I'd die for you
Even if you were the cause of my death

I see you at every turn
Hear you down every hall
Feel you like bugs crawling up my spine
Like a disease that can't be cured

You altered my brain chemistry
Now I must live the rest of my life
Feeling like a monster
When in reality I was just a kid
Who thought she was in love

<u>Love Too Young</u>

He told me that he loved me on my bedroom floor
He told me that he loved me and he didn't love her
And that all sounded like music to my ears
But we both kinda knew that it wasn't even real
And what I thought was love was really my own hell
It's hard to be alone in the nighttime because
It makes you feel unloved but at that time
we were too young
To be in love

<u>Drunk In Love</u>

Your love made my vision blurry
so I failed to see the signs

It burned its way down my throat
and set my heart on fire

Tears of love ran down my face
As pains and aches fade away

Your love was all I needed to make me feel okay

Even though I cried at night
And you always told me lies,

I still stuck by your side
Because you made me feel alive

But I need to stop these unhealthy habits
Even though they give me fire

As sip of you is like a sip of poison
Slowly taking away my life

<u>Umbrella</u>

Loving you was like loving the rain
It always had this certain beauty to it
Whether it was light and soft
Or rough and ugly
I would always find myself admiring it

But no matter how much I loved the rain
And all its natural beauty
It hurts my health to stand under it
But I can't just live my life
Loving you from under an umbrella

<u>My Nightmare</u>

I want to run away
Away from you while I still can
I don't care where I go
As long as I'm away from you
I don't have what you want
Or want to give up what I have
I was only just a kid
But you were too so is that okay
I only wanted your love
But you wanted to take control
I gave you all I had
And now I have nothing to give
I want to run away
To a place where I can sleep
Sleep away the pain you dealt
And hope my scars heal on their own

<u>Hold Me Tight</u>

I say I want your love
and you throw curses at me like sharp daggers
I ask for you to hold me close
and you hold my head underwater
I reach for your hand
and I am met with the cold shackles you bound me to
I tell you to let me go
let me be free
and the grip you have around
me only grows tighter
though I suppose this is what I get
for asking something so broken
to hold something so delicate

Until Death

I'll love you til the day
the sun no longer has its rays
but I can no longer wait for you to love me back
because every day that passes
I feel my soul slip away
reaching out for your hand
hoping you would reach back
but I stand blindly in the rain
where you left me alone
where I would die waiting for you
but when the fog lifts
all you find is the ghost of my love

<u>Thorns Of Love</u>

Please do not mistake my distance for betrayal
for I promised I would love you
for as long as the moon dances around the earth
the way you do with my heart
which now belongs to you
despite how you've left it to die out in the storm
I still love you like a rose to rain
but would rather choke on its thorns than tell you that

<u>Let Me Sleep</u>

You're all I talk about
all I think about
all I dream about
so much of you roams my body
despite your touch only being a memory
my heart and mind only belong to you
and if I could rip those tainted pieces out of me
I'd do so without a second thought
if only I could stop loving you
just as easy as you threw me away
perhaps I'd be able to sleep at night

<u>What The Heart Wants</u>

But as long as my heart continues to beat
I will think of you with every pulse
but I will not hesitate to carve my heart
out of my chest
if it meant I could get a quiet night's sleep
without it trying to break its way out
though my ribs to get to you

Karma Is Sick

You put me through hell
leaving me alone on the darkest nights
to fend for myself against your demons and my own
yet I wish nothing but the best for you
The only karma I wish upon you
is that every time you remember me
A bottomless pit fills in your stomach
and it becomes hard to breathe
as your throat closes up
despite the feeling of wanting to vomit
and there's a putrid taste in your mouth
that you can't get rid of
I hope every time you think of me
that you feel so sick to the point of death
but the reaper never arrives to claim you
and you are forced to live despite wanting to die
just as I once did for you

Could've Been Better

Perhaps I could have loved you better
if you had only shown me if you loved me at all
instead of keeping me guessing
of my worth and value to you and myself
perhaps I could have loved you better
if I knew you loved me at all

<u>Baby Steps</u>

Some days I feel myself getting better,
yet I can't shake the desire
of wanting to feel your skull crack under my boots
perhaps progress and peace are not one and the same.

<u>Burn For You</u>

I loved you so much,
I cradled your hate in my hands
and let the blood soak through my palm lines,
and it burned more than anything,
but darling,
I burned for you,
until I was ash,
I burned for you.

<u>Eternal Scars</u>

Your presence left a scar on my soul
so deep and sunken
yet bleeds as fresh as the day it was left
and I'll hold each drop of blood
in the hands of mine which yearn for yours
your presence left a scar on my soul
so how dare you tell me to just forget about you

<u>One Step Forward, Two Steps Back</u>

For a while, I was doing good, getting better, and feeling better
but I wasn't healed from the addicting idea that I needed to be
loved by someone
and by the time I realized that
I had already met you
who held me close and kissed me softly
and cared about my health
and got me flowers when I was down
all of a sudden I lost my independence
I lost my strength, my focus, and what little stability I had built
up
you make me feel weak
but you offered this protection like no other
and suddenly I didn't mind feeling so pathetic
as long as I could be so in your arms
and here I thought I was getting better.

You Make Me Crazy

When you stand there,
Just your smile is driving me crazy,
Staring back at me my mind is hazy,
It's not fair how you make it look easy,
And this feeling is driving me mad,
Making concentrating hurt really bad,
thinking back to the night when you had
Your lips on mine and I could no longer stand,
I need to leave but your touch is conflicting
with my conscious so I act on instinct,
Before I do I need to know if you're in this
or should we end this,
even if we choose to just stay friends,
Your smile drives me crazy to no end
When you just stand there.

<u>Another Broken Promise</u>

We promised we wouldn't get attached,

we swore we wouldn't become more than friends,

we said that each kiss was just for fun,

so why did you hold me so close that night

with gentle hands running up and down my back,

why did you kiss my forehead with such gentleness that I almost didn't feel it,

why did you treat me like something more than just casual,

why pretend not to care but fail to hide the emotion in your eyes,

why won't you just leave so I can fall apart and get over you already,

why don't you leave before I break another promise?

<u>Fever Dream</u>

You weren't my first,
and may not be my last,
but I will cherish every moment
that we had,
so please pretend to love me,
for just one more night,
feed into our desire,
hold me close tonight,
what we have is far from real,
please let me keep on dreaming,
I promise I'll wake up tomorrow.

<u>A Kiss On Marble</u>

The way you gently touch the
parts of me I can't see
making me forget
the way my scars still burn.
The way you whisper my name
like art inside a gold frame
I swear I won't forget
the nights you shared with me.
lips as sweet as caramel
like a kiss on marble
a stain that's permanent
I don't want to forget
the paint you pressed upon me
a canvas soft and empty
no way I could forget
the art you made of me

<u>Our Night</u>

Wanna feel the heat of your body rise
wanna hold your hands as we hit our high
wanna feel you close all throughout the night
as were on our own away from peering eyes
I wanna hide away with you in the night
as the moon and stars shine by our side
Don't fight the temptation, no separation
Don't be nervous just trust my touch
don't break the friendship on complications
it's easier if it's just us
no need for emotions
laced in shackles
its just lust

Entranced

You're all I see in this room
my northern star in the night sky
my heart beats for you
please place your lips upon mine
the way eyes possess me
make me forget how to think straight
but you hold me closely
the warmth you give ignites me
the way you consume my mind
I cannot sleep without you
I love the light you give
there is no one else like you

<u>Love Is Distant</u>

You look so pretty
Shining like the stars
I'll love you like the moon loves the sun
with its cold heart
Drunk off your light
In love with your smile
But I'll hide away each time you come around
Because someone like me
Can't hope to shine like you
Like you're the main attraction out of Hollywood
Because you're my star
So far out of reach
But I'll still love you from here
No matter how far I have to be

Don't Do This

For the love of all that's holy and sinful,
don't get close to me,
don't act like you care about me,
don't tell me you love me,
don't kiss my forehead or hold me like I'm worth something,
don't say you're different from everyone else when you're not,
and don't make me fall in love with you,
because as strong as I am alone,
I won't have the strength to fight you when you decide to leave
and because I care so much I'll still wish you nothing but the
best,
so please don't make me fall in love with you

Your Lust, Your Lies

If I could give you all of me I would
But I can't stoke this fire
My body bleeds for your arms around me
But something tells me to stop
I wanna feel the way your body moves
Only from my touch
But when the sun rises slowly at dawn
You will be gone
You try to coax me out of my insecurities
But I still hold them close
They're all I have protecting me
From love-infested wars
I want to give you all of me tonight
I know it won't mean more
Then drunken lust mixed with desire
So please don't lie

<u>The Things You Do</u>

Most nights I just think about you;
think about the little things you do
and it's been driving me mad,
dreaming bout all the nights we shared.
I can't help thinking about you,
the way you smile just makes me swoon,
and your laugh is my favorite too,
the way you hear it from across the room.
Usually, I stay away from boys like you,
because I know it'll hurt when you leave me soon,
but the night we danced together in the rain
made me forget the person I should be,
late nights full of drunken talks
into mornings where we're cuddled up;
I don't care if it's real or not
for tonight it's all I've got

<u>Why Do I Like You?</u>

You call me clumsy but I still like you
you say I drive you crazy but I still like you
You say you hate me but I still like you
You say I'm not your type but I still like you
You ignore my words but I still like you
You don't want me but I still like you
I do not know why I like you
But I'm in love with all you do
It'd be a lie to say I know you
but I wanna learn more
you are my muse

<u>You Own Me</u>

It's getting hazy now,
A high that won't come down
Your wandering fingers are what set me on fire
The moment I look deep into your eyes
Full of hunger that desires
I promise all of me; heart, body, mind, and soul
I promise I will never leave you alone
No matter how hard I try to run away
I don't wanna
'Cause leaving you alone cuts deeper
Then being on my own
I have no more control
It's getting hazy now
I don't wanna come down
If that means going to sleep all alone
The moment you look deep into my eyes
All you see is my desire
My soul belongs to you
And you belong to me
The way you are
it's the way you make me forget how to be angry
by filling me with so much light
but then make me want to rip my heart out of my chest
when you say I'm just a good friend
it's the way you smile at me right before you kiss
yet refuse to sit next to me when we're out with friends
it's the way you say you act like a jerk so I won't fall in love with you
but act so kind and hold me so close when it's just me and you

you drive me crazy yet I'm still crazy for you
and as much as I know I should quit
my heart just doesn't want to

<u>To Love Is To Learn</u>

I'll become anything you want me to be
if you want someone to dance with
I'll learn how to dance
and if you prefer to speak in Spanish
then I'll learn to do that too
I'll watch all your favorite movies
and listen to the music you like
but if what you want me to be
is a good friend to you
then I'll learn how to be that
while still loving you

<u>My Love</u>

I don't know how to love like everyone else
so instead I'll show I care the ways I know how
like making sure I have a full water bottle on me in case you
need it
I'll always tell you to be safe right before you head out and I'll
tell you to call me if you need anything
even though I don't have a car I'll find a way to get to you if you
need me
I'll be sure to keep the volume on my ringer loud and sleep with
my phone in hand just to be sure I hear it
and if I don't, I promise I'll wake up every hour just to see if
you texted me
I'll pester you to sleep giving up the bed so that I don't distract
you with my own insomnia
and I'll write poem after poem about the things I love about
you
sometimes writing with pen and paper
so I don't wake you with my excessive typing
I'll grow my nails out to give you better head scratches
even if it means having alternatives for dealing with my nerves
I'll keep notes saved of all the things you like and the stories be-
hind your scars
I may not know how to show my love the way you want me to
but that doesn't mean I don't care

Let Me Love You

The way your arms wrap around me
makes me feel alive and free
I promise I won't let you down
the way your eyes shine so bright
makes me fall in love every time
don't wanna look away or miss a thing
in love with the way you hold me
strong hands touch me gently
wanna feel your love for just one night

<u>My Muse</u>

You have become my muse.
The root of every thought racing through my head,
The memory of your hands on me still fresh in my mind,
I crave it like a drug as well as your lips on mine.
I spend countless hours writing about how you've plagued my thoughts
And I'll continue to type onto a dimly lit screen
About how your eyes are the perfect shade of brown,
And how I'm addicted to the way you kiss me.
I'll show my love the only way I know how
And that's through the work I live for now.
I'll spill my heart onto each key I type,
Not caring if my words lack sense
I'll write about you until the moon falls asleep
And the sun creeps through my window.
I'll then drag myself to bed holding the thought of you closer than the sheets around me
And when I fall asleep I promise you're my final thought
As you've given a poet a heartbeat again and for that,
you arc now my muse

<u>My Smile</u>

I hate men and I hate smiling
and I especially hate when men tell me to smile
but when you do it
when you look at me with those eyes and just say smile
I have to hide my fade in my hands pressing them close to my
cheeks to stop the smile from forming
but I can't
not when I can still feel your gaze on me
as you tell me smile again and I can just hear the smug expres-
sion on your face
yet I still find myself smiling around you and I don't understand
why
just like I don't understand why you tell me to smile in the first
place
and even though I still hate smiling
I guess hate it a little less when I'm around you

You Ruined Me

You completely ruined me
As I now spend my days writing about only you
And the emotions you fill me with
I find myself smiling at the thought of you while doing the dishes
And I hold my phone so close to me throughout the day
Just in case you decide to send me a text
you've ruined me to the point
Where I have to keep myself busy until I am exhausted
Because sleep no longer comes easy unless I am beside you
And the way I could trace out your features blind
As I now know your face better than my own reflection
Or how I'll stop my constant typing and continue my work on pen and paper
To make sure I don't wake you
It's the way you now completely ruined me
And I want to say it's in the best way possible,
But knowing you,
I'm not entirely sure yet.
The one I could never have
Sometimes I wish we'd met before the people we once loved tore us apart
Maybe then you wouldn't be scared to fall in love again
And maybe I wouldn't be so reluctant to trust you
But instead in this life
You'll only ever be the person behind every sad song I hear
The one who taught me about false hope and how much it could ruin someone
You're the reason I tell people love is just a word

You'll only ever be a small chapter in my life even if I could write a novel about you

But none of that matters anymore, the feelings I had don't matter anymore

despite how overflowing they were

Despite how much I wanted you

To be wanted by you

You'll forever be the one I could never have

<u>Love Kills</u>

I may love you but I hate you at the same time
the lies you tell fester deep inside of my mind
now my love poisons everyone in my life
like venom, you can see the dark in my eyes
telling myself I will be fine
as your plague chokes down all of my cries
when I die I'll know I was never enough
not enough for your sinister rides
or enough to keep you guessing all of the time
pure love was just never enough

<u>My Ring</u>

He kissed my hand
The hand I wore my ring
My ring which I promised myself
To never fall in love again
To never let anyone get that close to my heart again
Yet here I am alone with him
After falling asleep in each other's arms
Not wanting to leave the bed
Hoping the world beyond these walls
Will grant us a few more minutes
I realize now how much I've screwed up
How badly I've broken my own promise
As he kissed my hand just above where my ring sits
I felt that promise crack and hit the ground
I thought my ring would fall with it
Instead, it sits there on my finger
As he continues to hold my hand
I feel a pinch in my chest, in my heart

<u>Was It Love?</u>

Or was it the fear of how this love would eventually ruin me?
Almost perfect
He said and did all the right things,
He told me he loved me
Told me he missed me
Said he wanted to hear my poetry
Danced in the rain with me
Got me flowers when I was down
Held me close and kissed my forehead
Each night we shared a bed
And not once did he pressure me to do anything I didn't want
to.
He said and did all the right things,
He was damn near perfect,
But every moment we shared,
Every memory I have,
Each time I see him,
Not once has he been sober.
So in a way,
Not once was any of it real,
Was it?

Your Portrait

One night I sat alone in my room
As always my thoughts are only drawn to you
So I decided to focus my hand on painting
Hoping it'll be just as distracting
But as my hand glided across the canvas
I could only see you in front of me
And like my mind
My hand soon betrayed me too
As I could not stop them from thinking of you
Even with blurry vision I still could map
Your features like the back of my hand
From the scar above your eye
To the way your face softens when you smile
I end the night with a clear picture of you
Feeling betrayed by my mind
And the mess it usually is
The mess I usually count on to keep me busy on sleepless nights
like this
Was stuck entranced with the thought of you
So as the morning arrives I'll set off to buy more canvases
Because I don't think I'll heal from a sickness such as this

<u>I Love...</u>

I love how your eyes shine so bright against the city lights
And the way you smile at me when you make me shy
I used to think love was just a word
Until I met you who changed the meaning
I love it when you kiss me so softly and so gently
But hold me so tight you could easily break me
I love who you are when we're alone
And I hate who I am the moment you leave

<u>The Choice Is Yours</u>

You're the closest thing to heaven on earth;
with golden eyes and touch so familiar,
as if it's where I belong,
but with the way you speak and hold yourself,
so prideful and mean,
I often think I'm in hell;
that perhaps I've fallen for a lie
and with no desire to seek the truth,
I know you'll be the death of me, my dear,
and whether my soul goes to the light or the fire,
I believe that choice lies in your hands,
the same hands I cannot seem to pull away from,
the same hands I pray never let me go.

<u>Sweet Like Honey</u>

Sweetheart, I don't need much,
just look at me with those eyes,
whisper a few words laced with honey,
And I'm all yours tonight.

I'm Yours

You can remember as many details about me as you want
just at the end of the day
please forget my name
and call me yours instead
call me your love, your light, your beloved
even if it's just for tonight
let me belong to you

<u>Easy Is Never Easy</u>

I sit at my keyboard typing through tear-stained eyes
Because drowning in my work is better than waiting for you
I take longer naps throughout the day
Because it's better than waiting for you to text me
I delete our messages because it is better than rereading them
Trying to understand if what you said was real or not
I stay up for as long as my body will allow
Because it is easier than laying in bed all night thinking about you
I started convincing myself that everything that happened between us
Was just the alcohol making those decisions
And that all you said to me were just drunken thoughts
And all I was to you was someone to hold at night so you didn't get lonely
Believing we never had a chance, to begin with,
Is easier than thinking I wasn't enough for you
It is so much easier to hate you
But god is it hard to stop loving you.

<u>Hates' A Strong Word</u>

Perhaps I am hateful
because every time I hear your voice
I want to carve out my eardrums
each time you cross my vision
I want to drill screws in my eyes
knowing we share the same oxygen
makes me want to burn my lungs to ash
I would even go as far as to rip out my own heart
Because as strong as my hate may be
I fear my love for you is even stronger

<u>Baptize A Sinner</u>

All my life I have been labeled a sinner
but honey for you I would repent
as long as the holy water pours from your mouth into mine
I would happily drown in it
if it meant getting to kiss you just one time

<u>What Do You Think?</u>

Do you ever think the moon cries for the sun?
If so does the sun ever hear whose wails?
Or does the fire from which it burns,
Scream louder than the cries of the moon?
Does the sun even know the moon exists?
Do you even know I exist?

Frostbite Fire

A fire within me burns cold
but the light you cast
makes my solid blood run warm
in this eternal winter
you are my summer

<u>See Me</u>

But the sun saw how I admired you
and the stars gathered as I ranted endlessly about you
even the moon understood how I cried for you
the galaxy saw how much I yearned for you
so why couldn't you just see how I was there for you?

<u>Why?</u>

Why is it now I hate the one I once cared for so deeply?

Why is it now I hate the sound of your voice yet still listen to every word you speak?

Why is it now I scrub my skin raw in the shower after allowing your hands to roam my body?

Why is it now the mere thought of you makes me sick to my stomach?

As if all the butterflies have now become moths,

slowly eating away at me from the inside out

Why is it my heart still yearns for you yet is overfilled with hate for you?

-Why must the devil be so beautiful?

<u>Just For Tonight</u>

You can pretend to not care about me
and I can pretend to hate you
but tonight when I sit in the hall
and life starts moving too fast
please kiss me to stop time
and let my world revolve around you
Just for tonight

<u>For You</u>

Wanna be your muse,
Wanna be your truth,
Let me be your blood
Rushing warm through you,
Something you can't lose,
I'm the one for you,
Just for tonight
Let me drown in you,
Leaving me black and blue.

<u>Those Eyes</u>

You have such beautiful eyes,
so warm yet tragic,
like embers to a fire,
so pure and full,
like honey glowing in the sun,
yet you keep your distance like sworn vows
and I keep praying to get closer to your soul,
but I'll remain content with looking into your eyes,
as that is the closest to heaven
a sinner like me can reach.

<u>Deadly Silence</u>

I swallowed my words like full cubes of ice
plagued with frostbite
so you can remain warm
spilling your words like water on paper
running until there's no surface to claim
I drown in your words while choking on mine
and you don't even notice I'm dying

<u>The Last Exception</u>

I don't trust people yet I made an exception for you
but the night you had a hold around my throat
so tight
so full of anger
so suffocating
as my lungs weakened and my heart shatter
I could never look at myself the same after that
what did you do to me?
what illness did you infect me with?
and how the hell do I get rid of it?
-why me...

<u>Enough?</u>

I swallowed your lies like they were my final meal
I crossed my own boundaries just so you didn't have to travel
far
I may not have done it all
but I did what I could
why wasn't that enough?

<u>To Hell With Hope</u>

Part of me knew it would all go to hell
But I had hope
Part of me knew I would break
But I had hope
Part of me knew how this would end
But I had hope
At this point I want you to go to hell and take Hope with you
You are both good for nothing

<u>What Do You See?</u>

Do I look like summer to you?
Do I look free and warm and full of life?
Or do I look like winter?
Full of emotion and wonder
Do I look as beautiful as the seasons?
Or am I as blank as an empty torn canvas?
Do I look like anything at all to you?
Did I mean anything at all to you?

<u>Dance</u>

It takes two to tango,
but I didn't know I'd be dancing with the devil
paralyzed from the neck down,
you control my movements
bending me to your will,
I follow your voice like a siren,
you lure me close,
and I know full well this will be the end of me,
but my mind is far too gone to care right now.

Sink Or Swim

Your love is as vast as the Pacific
and often times I find myself lost at sea
trying to navigate my way to the
eye of the hurricane that is your heart
but as the days turn into nights
my raft crumbles more
from your harsh waves that beat and crash
though that does not sway me
for I will swim until you love me
or I will drown trying to prove it to you, my love

<u>Dear God...</u>

Dear god,
I think I'm in trouble
there's a boy
so pretty and pure like a cloud
but so full of rain it's almost frightening
and he shines so bright I would trade the sun for him
Lord, I am in love
but god does it scare me
with every prayer I have left
to the last drop of warm blood rushing through me
Please don't take him away from me
Amen

<u>You And Me</u>

With a little bit of me
and a little bit of you
in this neon-lit room
leave marks only we can see
Sharp wit from you
small bites from me
this world is only we
and nobody else will see
How were doing fine
like blood and wine
we mix like dye
it's only you and me
I can't see, but I can feel
I felt everything that night
it may have been too dark to see clearly
but the way his hand rested against my cheek
thumb grazing softly beneath my eye
slowly pulling me closer to him
not to kiss me
but to just hold me closer to him
I felt everything that night
and I no longer need to question what he feels for me
because no one can fake something that innocent
no one can fake something that real

<u>Do I Love Him?</u>

"But do you love him?"
They ask.

I love him,
I love him so much it hurts to breathe
but not as if I'm drowning
but as if I'm on top of Mount Everest
and I'm truly seeing the world for the first time

<u>Love From Hate</u>

You have ruined my life
in the best way possible
as I grew up with only hate in my heart
when I look into your eyes
I forget the meaning of the word
'hate'
as strong as the word love
a word so foreign to me
'love'
I hate how much I love you
But I love you more than hate could compare

<u>Sun-Kissed</u>

Silver burns and gold turns stale;
but the sun still shines so bright on you.

Angel Of Honey

Watercolor eyes painted of honey and gold
I cannot help but fall into a trance under your gaze
so pure yet hungry
it's immensely distracting
sending my stomach into a twist
wondering if your lips are coated
in the same flavor as your eyes
sweet like honey
as rich as gold
if offered the chance
I'd give all my earnings
for a single taste
for my angel of honey

<u>Burn Me</u>

You flicker like a fire illuminating a dark forest
so cold I watch idly as you set the green ablaze
tempted by your warmth I reach out my hands
open, scared, willing
resting them among your fire
you engulf me entirely
but I do not burn
Pathetic protection
I've spent my entire life learning how to protect myself
how to be alone
how to survive alone
but you offer this protection
that makes me feel pathetic
oh, but how safe does it feel to just fall apart in your arms

<u>Water Me</u>

But in the fire of my hatred,
a cooling peace rushed over me like water,
and I could finally breathe again,
in your oxygen so pure,
I could finally see again.

-you make me forget how to be angry

<u>Morning Doesn't Hurt Anymore</u>

And suddenly it was morning
and instead of wishing for the day to end permanently
I wished to fall asleep in your arms all over again

2

When Nights Are Restless

<u>Pretty In Red</u>

You could pierce my heart with a knife

And I'll still admire how beautiful you look

Stained in my blood

-Red never looked so pure

<u>An Open Wound</u>

I'll love you like an open wound
I'll tend to your every need
morning evening and night
only ever using a gentle touch
always keeping you safe from harm
I'll keep you warm from the cold
and give you clean air to breathe
I'll love you when you're fresh
I'll love you when you scar
and I'll love you when you heal
even if I get dirty in the process
or lose hours of sleep
I'll give all of my attention to you
for you are my open wound
a part of me whose pain feels personal
and since I can't take that pain
I'll ease it the best I can
as when I vowed to protect your heart
I vowed to protect your wounds too

<u>Wait For Me</u>

If I could lie here with you under the sky forever,

resting with the wildflowers who dance in the wind,

the wind that brushes against our skin,

our skin that's being kissed by the sun's rays; so full of warmth and love

just like you, my heart, who outshines it all

and I promise to one day rest beside you

so that we can be together forever more

no longer bound by the chain of the living and deceased

wait for me, my dear,

and we'll be one with the sky for eternity

<u>Love Is Poison</u>

Against her better judgment, she was in love.

In love with shadow-tainted clouds filled with sorrow and despair,

clouds that shed something thicker than blood and darker than oil

a sight most people would hide from;

but to her, it was as beautiful as a poem,

and as she admired them like an astronomer to stars

a few droplets began to fall landing in her big doe eyes

which she chose to keep open wide

not wanting to miss a single pulse

its poison spreading through her body

like wildfire tainting her mind and soul

sometimes she thinks it would've been best

if she just kept her head down

but against her better judgment,

she still fell in love.

<u>The Night Is Alive</u>

The air felt cool and crisp
As the wind danced through town
So quietly as not to make a sound
The streetlights loomed overhead
Casting a soft yellow glow like stars in the sky,
And the moon was gleaming at the earth
As if flashing its biggest, brightest smile.
And although the night is meant for all
I can't help but wonder if this presence is recurring
Or is it only a gift to those who wait to see it

<u>My Melody</u>

Her voice is as sweet as honey,
and her skin as soft as silk;
Her eyes cry tears of diamonds
and her smile is as warm as her embrace:
Her hair is always messy,
but in a way that looks intended,
and her nails are always jagged
from biting them while lost in thought;
She's a soothing melody with beautiful lyrics,
she's the song you'd always have on repeat;
She makes life itself feel like a music video,
one that I'd never want to end.

<u>Fly High</u>

When your wings get tired from rougher flights,
just know that I'll be there.
I'll keep you safe from all the evil thoughts
and nightmares in your head
I'll hold every single burden
that weighs heavy in your hands
I'll do what I can to see you smile
I'll stay on the ground to see you fly
I'll watch closely as your golden wings
soar high across the sky
I'll relight the match every single time
you start to lose your way
it's okay if you leave me
I just wanna see you free

<u>My Light</u>

She looks so pretty,
pretty like the city-
lights that shine
like midnight stars
dancing above all
a voice like honey
eyes of diamonds
a heart as pure as new freshly fallen snow
she owns my heart
my angel of the light
I'd give her all of me
if she asked me to

<u>Her Angel</u>

On her shoulder sits a devil
that has grown to be her friend
sending hate and angry thoughts
straight to her fragile head
but she doesn't listen to his words
or follow anymore
all she sees is the angel of her light
the boy she calls the love of her life
no longer does she feel the need
to have to fight the world
her angel by her side taking away
the heavy sword she holds
no more darkness in her heart
no more worlds falling apart

<u>100 letters</u>

He'll write 100 letters to her confessing his love
each one more poetic than the last
and his handwriting getting messier
with every word he scribbles
but the letters he writes are full of so much love
he could charge every star in the sky
keeping them alive for another century
each letter he writes to her
is another piece of his heart he'll gift her
and with no intentions of keeping it
hell write 100 letters more
100 more letters that at the end of the day
will never get sent to the owner of his heart
100 letters that'll sit in a box in the back of a closet
slowly forgotten about like a dying star
100 letters that perhaps if they were sent and received
could've kept a star alive for another century or two

<u>Goodnight</u>

He goes to bed early. Like super early. Like 8 pm early.
And as much as he says I need to get more sleep
he doesn't force me to go to bed the same time he does.
Instead, if he wakes up in the middle of the night
and notices I'm still not there,
He'll get out of bed with tired eyes
and come looking for me.
No matter what I'm doing
even if it's work-related,
He'll pick me and carry me to bed
and just to make sure I don't leave
He'll wrap his arm around my waist
Hold me close and say,
"Go to sleep idiot."
I tend not to argue or protest,
I just close my eyes and listen.
Because I know you're just looking out for me
Since I struggle to do it myself sometimes,
And I love you for that,
I love you,
"Goodnight"

Sun Walker

Follow the sun my dear, and she wont leave you astray
follow the light that burns from within you
as you were born among the stars
I will stick to the shadows of the moon
admiring from afar
content with the solitude I've been confided to

-you're so beautiful

<u>Quiet Fire</u>

She begs for time to pass as if it were the only god she believed in
she wished for the days to end sooner like a spoiled child on
Christmas
she cried for the pain to stop as if someone would hear her
yet she remained silent when someone asked how she was doing
for as angry as she was
she didn't know how to burden those around her
so she took her anger out on herself instead

<u>Shadow</u>

I always thought we were in this together
until I saw how bright the light inside you shone
I didn't see it at first
how I was dead weight along for the ride
And even when I tried to catch up
It was as if my feet were one with the ground
and I was forced to watch you succeed
time and time again
while I was pushed to the back of the crowd
I pushed down the feelings inside me that made me want to scream
and vomit
instead, I smile and tell you I'm proud of how far you've come
and I will continue to admire the light you cast
even if it means I have to be your shadow

<u>Fire</u>

As water streamed down his face
Washing away the black ash and soot
his diamond eyes pierced those below him
And a smile crept upon his face
Knowing at that moment he had won
He laughed and danced as the world went dark
The only light coming from the flames surrounding him
Illuminating the scars on his skin
He set the stage making the world know his name
Shouting the story of how he came to be
Telling them, like the past, he never died
And he'll show the world how flawed and ruined it really is;
By burning the mask to show what monsters lie underneath.

Dogs Cry On Rainy Days

This morning while I was on a walk I heard a dog crying
Most likely begging to get out of the cold rain
That had been going on all night
Its cries were filled with pain and plead
Just begging for someone, anyone to help it
But no one came as the streets remain empty
And each homes inhabitants lay asleep in their beds
Warm and safe without much care in the world
Something that poor dog could only dream of
Yet he still cried with any ounce of hope it could find
Its cries were so loud that they leaked through the music
playing in my headphones and dug into my soul
I wish I could've helped it but strangely enough
I never saw this dog once while I was out
Was it just around the next corner?
Was it locked up in a shed or cage?
Or was it just all in my head?
I still didn't have an answer 20 minutes after coming home
Only more questions with no answers
Like a dog needing help but no one being around

Fear The Fire

I often wonder if the moon ever fears the end of night
because of how suffocating the sun can be,
hogging the whole sky as if it were the only star in the galaxy,
granted the moon may get its light from that great ball of fire,
but I wonder if it would rather be dark forever
than inherit a trait from that narcissistic star

-why must my mother be so beautifully intimidating

Monsters Never Win

I'm running lost through the night,

Tree leaves and moonlight will guide,

My steps and wandering soul,

to find the way back home,

away from whispering lies;

Motionless faces they hide

Razor-sharp teeth and dead eyes

A modern nightmare inside.

Daydreaming of an end with solace,

no longer encased by darkness,

 I'll keep running faster and far,

I'll reach peace no matter how long.

<u>Broken</u>

My heart goes out to that broken young boy
Who was fueled by self-destructive dreams,
Who always worked to get stronger,
Even if his body couldn't take it;
Because the fire lit beneath him only grew hotter,
With flames growing brighter,
As his mind was consumed with power
He was eventually engulfed in the very flames
He once called his own,
But as the story goes, he never died,
Instead like a phoenix from hell, he rose from the ashes,
And is now back with a vengeance;
With scars marked up and down his body,
He wore them like trophies,
And presented them as his starting act,
Telling the story of how a weak, broken child
Who became the very monster he once swore to kill.

A Blanket For The Cold

As December closes in like the monster in my closet,
every night growing near baring its teeth and claws at me.

I find I do not have the strength to fight it off,
nor do I have the energy to run.

Instead, I shift over offering it a space on the bed beside me,
just in case it too, only desires refuge from the blistering cold.

However, if that's not the case,
then at least I won't have to worry about spending another Christ-
mas alone.

My Purgatory

She moves through the water with great ease,
the waves parting in her path
as the wind dances by her side;
her head holds high through the roughest tides,
and her grace reaches that of the sun
unafraid of those who dare challenge her strength;
for she owns the sea,
and with that my heart and soul,
as she is bound to these waters;
I am bound to her,
With a love so constricting of life,
too scared to be alone,
And as to keep a lover safe you keep a lover close,
sheltered from the rest of the world,
tied to the chains of love,
until the day she is consumed by the sea,
for she is not my heaven or hell;
but the in-between that'll drive any man mad
she is my purgatory

<u>Wind</u>

She carries the tears of those in pain,
And holds the fear of the ones who worry,
She hides the secrets of the ones in silence,
And sings melodies only the trees can dance to,
She flows so easily through life, always there, always aware,
Of the soft smiles shared in one field,
As chaos quickly brews in the next,
She continues to dance and sing,
Whether in peace and harmony or anger and rage,
She adds to the performance as a whole,
Making the audience remember every moment,
Even if she wasn't always visible,
She was there,
She was always there.

The Coward Star

I shout to the sun on dark stormy days,
calling it a coward for hiding behind its own tears,
while the innocent below are forced to face its wrath.
why does that egomaniac get to run and hide,
but I have to catch every tear that falls from my eyes in unsteady
hands.
If I have to heal my own pain,
why can't that so-called godly star do the same?

<u>Mourning</u>

Ever since he left,
she spends her days sitting at a grave;
he may not have died,
but he killed a part of her so dear,
she lost the love of her life,
along with her love of life;
so she made a home
around solitude and stone,
while the man who murdered her,
waits for her body to turn cold.

<u>Fallen Angel</u>

You were my light,
my smile,
my angel,
I believed you were the best thing about me;
you gave me a sense of belief,
the faith of my prayer,
I swore myself to you
on my hands and knees;
I gave up everything for you.

But alas I swore myself to the wrong angel,
the angel who fell hard,
who now makes his victims fall harder,
the angel whose love is an addicting drug,
the angel whose promises are hollow like his heart,
I fell for him and his lies,
I fell for the Morningstar.

<u>Can You Keep A Secret?</u>

Crows scream in erratic joy,
As soft green grass turns to blackened ash,
And starry eyes of admiration
Become clouded by tears and asphyxiation,
Innocent eyes fill with terror and fear
Secrets are kept by a ball and chain
While skeletons are locked away,
all clues have been wiped clean
like a rose fully plucked of its thorns.
Except for one, so lone and small,
a thorn that's been hiding for too long,
One last thorn I need to pluck.

The last bit of evidence left alive.
but I know you'll keep my secret,
Because whether you like it or not,
You'll be taking it to your grave.

A Sinners Funeral

They tied her to the stakes and set her body on fire
hoping to break her soul and the sins it holds,
the sin of not forgiving the hand that broke her,
the sin of having a voice so loud and unruly,
the sin of wanting to love anyone she pleases,
they wanted to burn away her sin of being human,
for while they believed man to be monstrous;
she believed it was a gift to be human.

<u>Sunshine Girl</u>

With a smile as gentle as her heart,
and eyes as sparkling as her laugh;
so bold and intelligent,
I can't help but admire her,
she's as beautiful as the sun;
so bright and pure,
like the fire, she burns,
which can ignite your soul,
in the best and worst ways possible,
my dear sunlight,
please continue to shine,
for as the moon glows in the light of the sun,
I too glisten brighter in the light of you.

<u>Tale Of A Warrior</u>

With hair that flows like a river through the wind
I wish to be carried in her arms
secure with love and scarred with strength
like a warrior of peace yet will fight like a god
she is who they tell tales about
among a blazing fire
almost as sharp and alluring as her
I am a simple child to think I could be like her
but must it be a sin to aspire to such freedom?
for she does not believe in conformity
why should I?

O' Death

I used to be afraid of death,

afraid of an ending I would never be prepared for,

but after that night when I was alone in a world full of life,

a figure of death crept by my side like a curious stray,

with no energy to live or care to die that night,

it brought me comfort knowing someone so loving and gentle was waiting for me at the end

I used to be afraid of death but when my time comes, I will greet them like an old friend.

<u>One Wish</u>

I often forced myself away from slumber,
as I would only dream of you,
so I'd sit below the stars,
and count each one I saw,
who offered to be my friend,
hoping it'd stop my tears from falling,
but more stars appeared in the sky,
moving quickly at the speed of light,
those stars offered me just one wish,
anything in the world they said,
but I told them I just wanted you.

<u>Too Hot To Handle</u>

She was simply human with the desire to be loved,
she held her heart to the sun, seeking its warmth,
but the glass organ shattered in her hands,
so from then on, she stuck to the shadows of midnight,
but you could still see her in the light of a full moon,
oh, how pretty she looked soaked in red.

-the sun who watched her break

<u>Little Lion</u>

little lion, little lion
it's okay to cry
don't look too deep in their eyes
all sheep are meant to die
close your eyes, open wide
take the first bite
before your soul harshly dies
take the hunters life

Pray In Red

The devil loves the petty god,
the one who clipped her wings so small,
no sun should shine upon her skin,
no clouds to touch,
no place to heal,
still, she'll pray in red for him to hear.

Her Death Row

She sits waist-deep in the chains of lead and steel,
her hands bound in spiked wire,
unable to understand why she is stranded,
drowning in air tainted by her own skin,
that rots and boils like her fermented eyes,
she can no longer see,
how she will be her own demise,
the death of herself,
fueled by spite,
as she believes if there has to be an end,
she will be in charge of it.

<u>Kill Me Or Lie</u>

Pull me apart like the petals of a rose,
scoop out my insides like the seeds of a pomegranate,
like ice cream in summer, watch me melt in your hands,
let me die in your arms to the sound of your heart,
but do not say you love me as all I ask,
for all I ask is for you to never lie to me.

Cinnamon Spirit

She haunts my house like a ghost made of cinnamon,
burning my lungs,
staining my walls,
heavy on my tongue.

So I scrub my skin until the walls bleed
I down whiskey to numb my mouth and throat
and swallow petals and thorns to open up my lungs.

But I still feel her within me,
haunting this house,
attached to my soul,
begging to be free
so she can finally drag me to hell with her.

<u>Death To The Youth</u>

I often hear voices leak from the attic,

mumbling and whispering like kids in a library,

and I hear their tiny footsteps

running through the walls,

giggles scatter around each corner I pass.

How I wish we were still that young and pure,

How I wish it didn't take us having to be killed to grow up.

<u>One More Day</u>

and suddenly it was 6 am,
and the neon-lit drive-thru had finally flickered dark
as the sun begins to peak through the horizon;
he couldn't explain how but the sun,
it somehow looked,
hopeful,
so he decides to make it a promise;
one more day.

-he'll give it one more day

<u>My Sins</u>

fill my heart with smoke in my lungs,
god, does it burn,
burn bittersweet,
filling my ears with bright blood melodies,
god, does it run,
run so warm,
filling my eyes with blue and white screens,
God, I can't see,
I don't wanna see,
please don't let me see what I have become,
blind to my sins,
my sins who are me.

<u>Red And Blue Make Purple</u>

A girl laced in red
loved a boy
who loved blue
so she gave him a bucket and brush
and he gave her marks of azure
yet it only mixed with her fiery hue
tainting her in shades of violet instead

   -it's a shame he hates the color purple

<u>The Fall Of Faith</u>

untethered, floating aimlessly
she grips tight to angel hair
yet tangled in the devil's tail
circulation cut off from her hands and feet
not sure what path to follow
she shuts her eyes tight
and waits for that final pulse to beat

<u>A Lie At Midnight</u>

a lie at midnight
is like a shadow in the dark
still being cast by the soul attached to it
but unable to see if it's as real as you and me
do shadows even exist in the dark?
can lies even be told at night?
like when you said I looked beautiful in my dress
but it was so dark I couldn't read your face
could you really see my dress?
could you really see me?
could you even see my shadow in the dark,
like a lie at midnight,
were you even there at all?

Don't Turn Around

I'll sip gas station coffee that burns bitter and raw
while listening to the radio tune in and out of signal
watching as the road ahead bubbles from the sun's heat
I force my hands to stay on the wheel and my foot to stay on the
gas
perhaps if I go fast enough, I won't have the chance to turn around
perhaps if I go far enough, I won't know how to turn around
and perhaps if I do turn around, I won't survive the drive back

-hopefully, I don't turn around

Old Home

The front door is rusted from the hinges
the roof cracked allowing the sun to peek through
and the windows are clear for birds and critters to come visit
the eggshell walls now littered with green and brown
the dinner table sits ghosts from the past
and in the beds the spirits of youth
a place that used to be known as home
is now one with Mother Nature
yet it's still more comforting than the fiery prison this structure
used to be,
hell,
my home,
hell on earth,
hell without the devil,
perhaps that's what this place has become.

War On Me

Why must you be so cold
freezer burns mark my soul
I've been drilling through holes
as my heart's been taking tolls
trying to make your parts whole

your tongue is a weapon
and my body on the battlefield
you lay waste and ruthless actions
on a field once so green and pure

but still to be your armor
I dare you to try to hit harder
for I will still be your blade
until my last breath fades

<u>It's 5 A.M.</u>

It's 4 am and I'm all alone
just like last night
and just like the night before
I watch the stars for signs of movement
listening for the front door to sound
but alas the night is filled with nothing but the wind
and the stars lie still in the sky
it's 4 a.m. and you're still not home
or perhaps your home just not with me
perhaps I've been waiting for a dream, losing sleep over an ideal
wishing for nothing but a fantasy
Now unsure of what my purpose is now
if not to wait for you, then for what
how do I fall asleep without you by my side?
how do I fall asleep alone with racing thoughts?
if you were even mine to begin with
If you were even real to begin with
It's 5 am and it's too late to sleep now
so I'll lie here wishing for your safety
as you may not be here and you may not be mine
 my heart still belongs to you, so I hope you slept well my love
and I hope you make it home safely tonight.

<u>I Miss You</u>

I miss you.
I miss your cold deep eyes.
I miss your rough yet gentle hands.
I miss hearing your voice.
I miss your never-ending teasing.
I miss our back and forth arguing.
I miss our long talks.
I miss your over protective nature.
I miss always competing with you 24/7.
I miss you talking about your favorite novels.
I miss your stuttering when you get flustered.
I miss everything,
From our loud and happy moments
to the sad and silent ones
To moments where neither of us felt strong.
but at least we were together.
I miss all of that,
I miss us, I miss you.
If only life didn't keep us apart

To: a memory
From: my heart

<u>Silhouette</u>

Sometimes I forget that you aren't here anymore
But it still feels like you are from time to time
I still wait for you to come home every evening
And I still wait for your frequent texts throughout the day
Updating me on how things are going
There are even times where I think I see you
out of the corner of my eye
When in reality it's just somebody else entirely.
At the end of the day
I know it's just my mind playing tricks on me
And I know you're never coming back
But it's not like you were ever here in the first place
Nonetheless, it still hurts and now all I'm left with
is your silhouette and fading memories

<u>Partners In Crime</u>

slowly I'll get you drunk off my touch
way stronger than the vodka
I'll have you lying with me in my bed tonight
just know I'm no naive young child
love isn't real in this world
I want to feel your warmth and your fire
so dance with me all night
all you want is to feel good
and I can do that for you
so just let me in
I swear you won't regret it
I'll be your Harley Quinn
as long as you're my joker
no monsters can touch us

Love Varies

When I fell in love it was completely unexpected and strange.
like taking that first sip of coffee in the morning
or when the first snow falls in winter.
And even though he can look cold and mean,
Being with him feels like being out in the sun and
having its rays warm your skin in a tight embrace.
A day of cleaning would turn into a mini-concert in the apartment.
And when it came to cooking and doing dishes that all became a competition.
But I'd loved every second of it and at the end of the day,
his rough hands danced with mine
And they never left each other's side.
He helped me see that love comes in many different forms
All you need is the right person by your side to experience it with you.

<u>Lucid Dream</u>

I still remember him like a lucid dream
Pretty eyes, pretty smile, pretty freckles
I knew the dream wouldn't last forever
I knew I would have to wake up eventually,
But I still chose to believe with all my heart and soul
that it was real
I chose to believe his lies
Then one day I was forced to wake up
leaving me alone again
and as tragic as it sounds
I can't wait to go to sleep tonight

<u>Open Door</u>

some days I see you pass by the kitchen window
and see your face through the peephole
so I leave the door unlocked at night
just in case you come home
but instead, a shadow creeps in and takes a piece of me each night
and when I wake in the morning
I recognize myself less and less in the mirror

-I don't remember how to lock the door

3

When The Mirror Is Blurry

<u>My Prison</u>

I am a prison to my own abyss,
no longer bound to the chains of pride and grief,
for I do not have the energy to care for such things anymore,
alas the loss of my shackles did cost me something dear,
my creativity, my ambition, and my energy deplete as quickly as
water drying in the sun,
and I can no longer find the strength to live like an ordinary hu-
man,
instead, I find solace in my loneliness,
though at the end of many nights,
I shatter like the glass meant to hold my tears,
for I feel more worthless when I am free.

<u>Sleep Does Not Come Easy</u>

As I toss and turn grasping for sleep,
I often dream of what it'd be like
to not go to be alone,
I dream of falling asleep
tangled in a set of arms,
no longer in search for warmth,
then my mind begins to wonder
if I even deserve a love such as that,
or am I bound to my work like a horse,
and forced to die like a fly on the wall
without any meaning,
am I forced to live without any meaning?
or am I forced to live with meaning deemed by another?
is that a part of love?
if love is even real at all,

-I should get some sleep but I can't stop thinking

Flawed Art

I am a form of art created from madness and delusion,
and people praise me like an abstract piece romanticizing my in-
ability to be understood,
but when the lights are off and the room is barren of souls,
I'm just a piece of work who only believes she's art when someone
else convinces her so,
but in the late hours of the night,
when it's just me and my flaws,
how do I convince myself I have any worth at all?

Unlucky Child

I stopped visiting my teenagers' grave,
As I no longer have the energy to leave my bed,
but among the sounds of monotone beeps and dark screens,
are the cries of my child begging for me to get up,
to visit the part of me that died a long time ago,
and I can't stand the thought of leaving that little girl alone,
but how do I turn off that machine so she doesn't hear me flatline too,
no little kid should have to go through that.

- I shouldn't have had to go through that

Anger Settles

"If you grew up with an angry soul in the house, there will always be an angry soul in your home."

But I was just a little girl,
I was just trying to understand,
I just wanted to help,
why does everything reek of irritation now?
why can't I stop shaking?
why couldn't I just be your little girl?
why do I have to be so angry?
and why must that anger be the only comfort I know?
I was just a little girl
and after all these years,

I still feel like a child.

<u>The End...</u>

When I can no longer lift my pen,
or raise my fingers to my keyboard,
know that my book has come to an end,
and incomplete or not,
please let me go peacefully,
for I'll be too tired to fight you anyway,
I'll be too tired to keep living anyway...

<u>Peace Is Sweet</u>

If peace were offered on a silver platter,
I don't think I'd be able to stomach it,
I imagine the taste would be sweet,
so sweet it's almost gut-wrenching,
and I don't believe my mouth is made for sweet,
I don't believe I am made for peace.

<u>My Blood Is Cursed</u>

An apple is as rotten as the tree it falls from,
and a tree is as poisoned as the soil it grows from,
I have been cursed with tainted DNA;
forced to infect those who try to devour me
with just one bite.

-trauma is inherited

<u>Acid</u>

There is a fire inside me that burns so foul,
like a chemical tainting my lungs,
I can hardly breathe anymore.

All she wants is to be loved,
please someone save her,
I can hardly breathe anymore.

  -she's just a little girl

<u>Crowded Company</u>

In a cemetery of misery,
I am kept the most company,
for as quiet the sadness may be,
it is always so damn crowded in here.

<u>Hereditary Storm</u>

I've never seen my Father and Peace in the same room together,
the man's eyebrows are in constant furrow,
and shoulders are always so tense,
like he's waiting for a deadly storm to hit,
but it never comes,
even when he swears it's near,
and as his daughter, I fear I am succumbing to the same fate,
to live in constant fear of the haunting storm,
though I'm not sure if I'll be strong enough to fight it when it comes.

<u>Writers' Sickness</u>

Trying to break writer's block is like trying to get myself to throw
up,
I stick my hand down my throat and reach for the emotions I wish
to reveal,
but often times nothing comes up,
though when I do reach back far enough,
I'm only able to pull out a few jumbled words and letters,
so with blurry vision and a twisted stomach,
I put the words together in hopes they make sense,
even if it takes me hours to do so,
I will gladly go to bed exhausted, nauseous, dehydrated, and with
tear-stained cheeks
if it means getting that disgusting bug of emotions out of me.

<u>December Blues</u>

and suddenly it was December;
and I can't find a single reason for wanting to see the new year.

The Monster In The Mirror

Drunk off the seclusion I have succumbed to,
I rant to the figure in the mirror in hopes of it understanding me,
but when I catch its gaze,
I am only met with pencil-dull eyes
that have no color to saturate them,
the figure looked like something out of a horror comic drawn by a
psych ward patient,
sunken cheeks, disheveled hair, pale skin,
that thing looks to be on the verge of death,
I close my eyes and ignore the knife in its hand,
perhaps if I go to sleep,
that monster will end itself.

<u>Peace Of Night</u>

I hardly can recall moments when I was proud of myself,
but when I'm sitting on the roof,
my gaze lost among the stars,
I feel my chest expand,
and my problems don't seem so suffocating now,
and for a moment,
life doesn't seem so bad.

-Night Owl

Handle With Care

Please don't hurt me,
because as guarded and independent as I am,
I can't help but offer you my heart,
and no matter how many times you strain it,
and bruise it,
and smash it,
and break it,
I will still offer it to you
after piecing it back together with my own clotted blood and tears
of salt,
I will still offer it to you,
hoping you'll treat it with care,
so please don't hurt me,
because I'll stay until the day
my heart stops beating.

<u>One And Only</u>

I do not know how to love peacefully,
for all I know is pure devotion and obsession,
to love one is to see one and only one,
even when the world is engulfed in flames,
they are the only one standing,
untouched from the flames,
for if a single flame scarred their body,
I would hunt down every god there is,
and destroy their world
for daring to harm mine.

Roam The Night

I wander under the stars with a face drowned in tears,
because if I were to run under the sun,
I fear I will be the next Icarus
and burst into flames trying to reach that star of fire,
for at least the moon with listen to my woes,
instead of burn me to death for having a heart.

<u>Bad Apple</u>

No matter how many breaths I took,
I could not stop the tears from falling,
so I sunk my teeth into my wrist
so I would stop crying at the thought of you,
the pain I felt in my punctured skin distracted me from the pain in
my heart,
the liquid that poured from my flesh gave me a reason to focus my
vision,
and the rotten taste I left in my own mouth reminded me
how I could never be the apple of someone's eye.

<u>Sharp Claws</u>

Everything I have ever let go of has claw marks on it,
except you,
you are the only thing I let wall away,
because the thought of leaving such an ugly scar on you
hurt more than watching you leave,
so I sit alone wrapping bandages on my arm.

-those claws had to go somewhere

Terminal Or Internal

I'm as healthy as I can be,
Yet I'm severely ill
In the desire of wanting to be ill
Just for someone to treat me
so tenderly and with love
I desire to be ill
So someone can care for me
the way it's seen in movies
I desire to be ill just to test the theory if someone cares at all,
But I also desire to be ill so I can finally have an excuse to rest
without being the one to pull the plug,
I may be healthy,
But I fear my illness is terminal,
And I don't think there's a cure for me.

<u>Anti-Touch</u>

Please do not lay a hand on me,
no matter how gentle,
I fear even the lightest brush against my skin will cause it to rupture,
and my blood will soak through like oil,
and I won't be able to stop it from spreading,
so please be cautious,
as I am not dangerous,
I just fear being in such danger again.

Like Mother, Like Daughter

My mother often sits in my room to vent about her pain,
and when she asks me about mine I remain silent,
for she does not know how to listen,
and I do not know how to speak.

-Perhaps I am more like my mother than I thought

<u>Imaginary Friends</u>

My anger laughs heartily as it throws its head around
nearly gouging out my eye with its jagged antlers,
and my grief cries rivers that drown my feet,
but I couldn't care less as its screams are more concerning,
and above them, my creativity watches me close with bloodshot
eyes,
I still do not know what it desires,
these are the only friends I've grown to know,
yet they tend to try to consume me most nights,
but I suppose none of us are perfect.

<u>Hope</u>

All it took was a moment too pure,
for my heart to beat too fast,
and my thoughts to run too far,
thinking someone like you could truly love me.

-the hopelessly hopeful

<u>Survival Procrastination</u>

She held the pen tight in her hand
writing so hard the paper beneath nearly ripped in two,
and perhaps if she held that pen tight enough,
she won't be able to reach for the blade
that wait across the desk for her.

-Hopefully, she doesn't remember her left hand is free

<u>Eye Of The Hurricane</u>

My eyes begin to water but not softly like raindrops off a flower,
but rather they want to pour and crash like a hurricane,
and you'd think you be safe in the eyes of that hurricane,
but I am afraid I am not that well-tuned,
as within my eyes is the closest you'll get to my soul,
a soul that's shattered in stained glass,
and bleeds like ink on fabric,
a soul that's hungry but can never be fed,
a soul that's tired but can never sleep,
in the eye of my hurricane is the worst place to be,
so when telltale signs of a storm begin to show,
take shelter immediately,
for I do not wish to hurt those who try to admire my disastrous
nature.

<u>An Innocent Dose</u>

Addiction runs through my veins,
so I stay clear of drugs and substances,
but I can't seem to stop myself
from seeking attention and validation
from those whose words are laced with honey and lust.

<u>In My Blood</u>

Why must I be human?
Why must I eat and sleep?
Why must I desire love and adventure?
Why must it be in my blood to live?

If it were up to me I'd drain my body every night
of the blood it holds just so I could sleep.

Self-Chore

The grief I hold weighs heavy in my arms,
crying like a hurt child,
the isolation I've become trapped in suffocates like guilt,
the anger that rests upon my shoulders sends aches through my body like an earthquake,
and the lessons I have learned scream reminders in my head of who I should be,
but my reflection remains ever blurry,
and I can't seem to hold my head up anymore
trying to take care of myself feels more like a chore I can't be bothered to do anymore.

   -I'm so tired

<u>A Strange Kind Of Tired</u>

I'm so tired, but not sleepy,
I want to rest but I'm not allowed to die.

So I'll continue to walk this earth with tired eyes,
and heavy feet waiting for the day that will be my last.

I don't wait for death,
I only desire peace.

<u>Home Alone</u>

I wanna go home,

to my room of pretty lights that bring my life color,

to my two screen monitors that keep me focused,

to my bed crowed with pillows and blankets where I can hide away

from the world,

to my loud music that drowns my thoughts,

I want to go home so my solitude,

I want to go home alone,

I want to be alone.

<u>One Reason</u>

The cold bites as hard as a wounded dog,
and my eyes sting as harsh as the words you spill,
I want to run my wrists under hot water
just to feel the sensation I desire so much,
but several reasons stop me from doing so,
but lord give me a reason to do otherwise,
and I will not hesitate to pick up this old habit
like a lucky penny off the ground,
just one reason is all I need.

<u>Deadly Appetite</u>

The way my stomach growls in hunger
deafens my will to think clear
screaming for the desire to be full,
but no matter how much it takes
it still screams for more
which I can't give,
so I fall asleep restless to thought
that I might be its next meal
and if that proves true
I know even that won't be enough to quiet it.

<u>Wrong Reflection</u>

I don't know what I look like.
So I stare into the mirror hoping for an answer,
But instead of finding a light in the tunnel,
I begin drowning in a pool so full of emptiness
I don't like what I see,
I don't like how I look.

-Why is the mirror so blurry

<u>A Million Stars</u>

On nights I feel my scars sting,
and soul weigh heavy,
I lay back and stare up at the stars and moon,
suddenly I feel less alone.

Internal Betrayal

Oh honey,
how could anyone love you,
when the person in the mirror can't bear to look at you

-the specter staring back

<u>Tear And Tear</u>

When my nails get too long
and chip slightly,
I tear the rest off,
like a piece of bark that slowly chips off an old tree,
I want to keep tearing until the tree is bare of its protective layer,
I want to tear off my skin until
only the muscle and tissue are what can be seen,
perhaps then I'll be more beautiful.

<u>In My Head</u>

I never leave the house without a loaded gun,
I never leave the house without 6 + 1,
7 times a day I will end it all,
in my head is where I fall.

7 times a day is when that gun is shot,
7 times a day I watch my body drop,
one shot is all it takes,
just to get my way.

But when I make it home,
the gun is quickly locked away,
because I can't afford to lose just one round.

I Just Want To Feel

My body shivers and trembles,
but the wind chill offers such a comfort
I can not find anywhere else,
like a lost stray looking for scraps,
I search for any ounce of love
to fill my bottomless pit of a stomach,
so hollow and empty,
like the eyes that stare at me from what is supposed to be my re-
flection,
but I shatter the glass with my fist,
and watch it all turn red,
I feel my lungs fully expand now
as my icicle ribs finally crack,
I feel something,
at last, I feel something.

<u>Your Wish</u>

And the doctor said to,
"Take this pill"
you'll look much better,
with a tiny waist,
and flatter stomach,
you'll get with any guy, no trouble,
when you give yourself to him.

Just one piece,
some pain,
his pleasure,
"Or you will be alone forever"
it'll hurt so much more,
but this is what you wished for.

<u>Hell On Earth</u>

My hands hang heavy as the heart I hold beats slowly,
Slowly my throat tightens as my blood rises to my tongue,
My tongue that has been burned to silence my words,
My words which they refuse to hear,
but hear me they will when I crush the dying heart in my hands,
my hands they will die by,
and I will eat their souls,
I will drag them down to hell and burn with them for all eternity,
for if they choose to call me a devil,
I will show them a darker hell
then the lord could ever conjure.

<u>Killer On The Run</u>

Who's that I see
 in the mirror
looking at me
with dreary eyes
blood on its hands
is it mine
how can I die
yet feel so alive,
how can I live as a killer on the run
tied down by guilty memories
but never have I felt so free,
a killer of mercy
I killed to release
my own soul trapped
by who they wanted me to be.

<u>I'm Only Human</u>

I have no inspiration,
no motivation,
I am nothing,
at the end of the day,
when it is just me and the moon,
I am not even a poet,
just a lonely soul with no one to talk to,
and emotions rampaging through my veins,
sometimes I forget I am only human,
and more often I'll forget that being human isn't a flaw.

<u>Isolation</u>

I hate getting attached to new people,
because no matter how long it has been,
no matter how healed I think I am from the past,
the second someone decides to leave
I find I am 11 years old again
sitting in my room alone
as tears and ink hit the floor like hail,
I'm forced to wonder what it is I did wrong,
or why I wasn't good enough for them,
or wonder if it's just my DNA to be unloved,
and if that is the case,
then how do I tell that 11-year-old
who's afraid of being alone
that we're going to be stuck that way forever,
and how do I convince her that it's not her fault
when I can't even convince myself.

<u>The Moons Gaze</u>

The hours of the day fall short
to all it is I desire to do,
so like an owl, I wander the night
using the moon's illuminating gaze
to drown myself in my work,
A hundred stars scattered above triple
in my haze of exhaustion,
for the sun may know my dreams,
but only the moon has seen my ambition.

<u>My Kitchen, My Power</u>

I have a set of tasks that I do at the end of the day.
I'll load the dishwasher till it's full,
Set the coffee for the morning,
wipe down the stove and sink until it's spotless,
And clean the counters even if they aren't that dirty,
I do this every day, 5 days a week,
sometimes on weekends if I have time.
I do this because in a life where I feel I have no control,
It feels nice to end the day knowing that the kitchen is clean
because I decided that it would be.
Even if it only lasts for one night
and I'll have to do it all over again the next day,
I at least get to go to bed with a sense of clarity
knowing that I got something done that wasn't an assigned task
or had a due date behind it.
So I may not be able to control everything in my life
but I can control whether or not
my kitchen gets to end up clean at the end of the day.

<u>My Crown</u>

If I could I stay here forever hidden away from the rages of war
outside these walls,
I'd spend eternity in your arms,
but we both know that would be an illusion,
an illusion that had to be killed,
driving the knife through their back was easy and smooth,
as if I'd done it 100 times before,
Because I know I'd do it 100 times again,
their body fell like a feather on the floor,
like a dream turning to dust as soon as one awakes,
I gather my crown, my strength, my weapon, and all,
and exit this dream towards the raging battle awaiting outside for
me,
The next time my crown is removed,
will be the day that I battle the reaper.

<u>Lone Flame</u>

I'm still breathing light,
Without oxygen, I will keep flying,
I'm kicking up ash,
As I burn hotter than the fire,
Set ablaze beneath me
Winning is all that I see
Failing is impossible
When you breathe nothing
But icy,
cold words that keep them as close as a fire,
That burns in a tundra left alone to die,
It's me standing in the freeze,
Me standing all alone,
Me on this cursed throne,
All alone in the freezing cold,
One day at a time,
I will survive,
From the fiery flames where I nearly died,
So I'll learn how,
To live for myself,
Even if that means having to learn to live on my own.

<u>Bad Luck</u>

No matter how careful I try to be,
There are still cracks on every sidewalk,
And broken glass trailing close behind me.
Four leaf clovers seem to fall apart at my touch,
And black cats always cross my path.
I'm attentive with my words but
They still come out wrong.
I plan my days ahead of time
yet still get rained on days meant to be sunny
I try to be careful,
I try to help others,
I try to plan ahead,
And I try to be the best I can be.
But I don't know how to
when I keep getting placed
at the bottom of the scoreboard.
Is it a severe case of bad luck,
or am I just unlucky?

Blurry

Words on a page slowly blend together,
As bedroom walls show strange faces,
My body sways back and forth,
Making movements I cannot control.
My arms feel heavy,
My face feels numb,
Is it all the caffeine?
Or maybe lack of sleep?
The sun is slowing rising so I can't sleep now,
And my project is due in an hour so eating can wait,
Just one more paper then I'll be done
At least till Monday, I can say I won.

<u>Solo</u>

Maybe I'll just stay alone,
staying focused on my goals,
dressing best and for success,
As I am nothing like the rest,
and they all keep on talking ill,
laughing like I will not kill,
but they don't know where I am from,
keeping track like stars above,
I'll remember who was with me,
and those of you who wanna be me,
don't need love from anyone,
not when I am on the run,
on the road, this race will win,
from each fight, I'll count the sin,
add them to my crown of jewels,
in the palace of my rule,
I'll stand alone without a care,
watch me, I am almost there.

<u>If I Could Do Anything</u>

What would I do if nothing was holding me back?
no mortal needs to eat or sleep,
no responsibility to uptake for society,
if I had the freedom of a god,
with the mind of an imaginative child,
and the heart of someone who had never been broken,
what would I do if there were no one holding me back?
no memories that haunt like shadows,
no scars that hang heavy like shackles,
if my spirit had been untainted by the world,
what would I do?
who would I be?
how could I live?
without the pain of being human,
how could I exist with such dangerous territories of freedom?
and how long before my reckless actions ruin the lives
of those who are tied down by the safety of mortality?

Little Miss Forgettable

Hello there, don't be lonely,
I'll fill the silence with melodies,
hello again, no need to know me,
I am little miss forgettable.

I'll hold your hand,
pretend to be your friend,
until the bell sounds or sunrise,
I'll be your friend,
until you leave me,
that's why I'm little miss forgettable.

Find your voice,
or seeking peace,
I'll be there right there beside you,
until you move on,
find another song,
I'll still be little miss forgettable.

<u>Family Genetics</u>

I love my parents,
but when I grow up I hope and pray I do not become like them,
I love my parents more than anything,
but I won't take their pain from them if I could,
because as an only child, it's my job to heal their trauma while also
handling my own,
I love my parents more than anything in this world,
but I'm a dark poet who doesn't believe in love anymore.

Enough Is Never Enough

"When will I finally be enough?" I ask.

"Once you do the impossible." They said.

"What is the impossible then?"

"Well that's you're job to find out," they said.

I don't see myself as "enough" until I am impossible,

I work from sunset to daybreak,

I count calories in meals

And exercise til I can't feel,

My arms or legs.

I look in the mirror and don't hate what I see

But still not happy with the results.

I'm stuck in an endless cycle chasing a goal that's not really there,

While not making any progress at all.

It's like trying to upload Windows 200

On a 30 year old computer,

And that update doesn't even exist.

So at the end of the line, with my final breaths, I ask,

"When will I be impossible?"

"Never," they said.

<u>Daily Chores</u>

I take pride in completing my daily chores.
cleaning around the house because I am responsible and happy,
not distracted.
but I have to leave the dishes for someone else to do
after noticing the knives that rest in the sink,
but the house won't be clean if I leave the mess there,
but I know once the water starts to run I won't be able to resist,
although my day won't be complete if the dishes don't get done,
The breath I now pull feels heavier than the last,
and my mind starts to spin out of control,
I need to feel better,
I need to feel something,
the completion of my chores,
or the satisfaction of spilled ink,
I don't care at this point but I know I should,
so I lower my head deciding to go back to sleep,
perhaps I'll try again tomorrow,
hopefully, the dishes will be done by then.

<u>Starved</u>

I was never served love so delicately on a silver platter,
instead, it was plastered on with a bandage by the same person,
whose words and touch cut deeper than the knives in the kitchen,
love was an apology after being degraded down to nothing,
but tears, dust, and self-hatred,
love was not being able to recognize yourself in the mirror,
because you changed everything about yourself,
to be good enough in the eyes of others,
love was spending every night alone wondering,
if they were going to come back,
love was wondering what you did so wrong,
to make them not even look at you for weeks,
love was dark, painful, disgusting, and burned going down your
throat,
like the shot of whiskey you'd take to numb your bleeding soul,
I may be young but I no longer believe in love,
because if what I lived through was love,
then I'd rather spend the rest of my life alone
than starve myself to death for something as rotten as love.

<u>To Live Again And Again</u>

If reincarnation is real,
perhaps that is the reason why
I look into the mirror
and don't recognize the face starring back at me,
perhaps that is the reason why I feel my
passions and desires are never truly my own,
and if reincarnation is real,
then perhaps I was successful in another lifetime
which would explain my desire to be great in this one,
although I suppose that means there were lifetimes where I ended
as a failure,
and perhaps that is why I fear the idea of being nothing,
if reincarnation is real,
I wonder how many lives you get before it's truly over,
because as much as there is I strive to do,
at the end of the line,
my tired soul only desires peace.

I Am An Artist

As an artist, you never stop working,
With thoughts constantly filling your head,
You strive to get it onto paper
and forge those thoughts into art
and that art into a masterpiece
To the point where you nearly go insane, and that's just the begin-
ning,
Because being on the brink of insanity to make an amazing piece,
You could easily fall into a limitless space,
Or you could work yourself to the bone to bring your work to life
To the point where you put your blood, sweat, tears,
and even madness into it.
And that's what makes a beautiful artist,
that's what makes me an artist.

Only Ever Ordinary

What makes me different from everyone else?
It's not my pain because everyone has struggles that's part of being human.
It's not being a writer because there are so many who have come before me.
It's not being a woman because there are stronger more inspiring women out there.
Why is it that everything about me that's supposed to make me unique just makes me seem so ordinary?
How is it possible to be unique in a world of 8 billion other people who are unique in their own way?
At what point does authenticity become a carbon copy in a different font?
At what point does being human mean just as little as being alive?

<u>Bad Dog</u>

You do not want me,

like a stray dog you look at me in pity

And decide all I need is love and affection,

until you get too close,

move your hand too fast,

or raise your voice just one octave,

and I bite you like the scared dog I am.

You'll throw me back out on the street cursing my name,

You do not want me,

I never had love served to me on a silver platter,

so I won't know how to love you at the end of long days,

You do not want me,

because like the stray dog I am,

I know you'll eventually tire of tending to my ugly scars,

and you'll want to move on to a pet with a clean coat and the abil-
ity to love,

you don't want me.

I'll do more harm than good even when I try to be enough at the
end of the day,

like a bad dog,

I'm the one who bites.

Tree Of Life

When I die bury me in a field of wildflowers,
so my heart can finally blossom like the aching seed it is,
and maybe one day if this tragic world doesn't end itself,
my heart can grow into a tree so tall that it could touch the stars,
so lush and strong with the life it once had,
to be a shield from the sun's burning rays,
and to support midday naps,
maybe then someone will finally see,
my heart for its beauty rather than its pain,
maybe then someone will finally love me.

<u>My Mirror</u>

It wasn't until I met him that I realized how damaged I truly was.

He was just like me and I was just like him,

From the stubborn attitude and sharp tongue,

To the way we explode when we finally reach our breaking point,

We get high off adrenaline and tear ourselves apart to win.

It's almost like we're carbon copies of one another,

We both put the weight of the world on our shoulders,

but still keep people at arm's length,

Maybe even farther than that.

Things are just easier that way.

We have a busy schedule,

Things to do,

Goals to reach,

Limits to push past.

I mean it's almost like looking at a mirror when I look at him.

He was just like me and I was just like him.

Villain Or Survivor

My sadness builds up behind my ribs to the point
I feel them crack a little more with each tear I shed,
and my happiness tingles in my hands and feet
causing me to bounce around like a small child.

But my anger floods my veins through my whole body,
some days I use it as a shield against sharp-fanged words
and other days I use it to get myself out of bed,
my anger isn't a beautiful storm you wait for to pass
but simply the reason I am still alive.

The only reason I want to be better is so I can prove I am better,
not like a villain but instead a survivor,
although I understand why people confuse the two,
yet I don't plan on changing anytime soon,
I can't heal the thing that's kept me going for so long,
I don't know who I'd be without it.

Poems Not For Me

Why is it that most poems are fueled by love or heartache?
Why is it that I can never find a poem about the anger that festers
inside someone?
About the fire it ignites in your stomach,
or how its pressure builds up in your head making you cry,
which aggravates you even more.
Why is it when I want someone or something to hear and match
my rage?
I only find those who empathize with me softly
and try to cradle me in their arms like I need love,
When all I need is to vent my anger rather than suppress it.
I want to feel my vocal cords tear from my screams,
I want my knuckles to burn and my breathing to be unsteady.
I want to feel the fragile furniture in my house crack and shatter in
my hands,
I want something to bite back at me,
And remind me that I'm human.
But it is 3 am and I need to be quiet
so I listen to music in my headphones loud enough to damage my
hearing,
and write until my pen tears through my notebook,
because every poem I find is about love and heartache,
something I don't care to feel anymore.

Pain Isn't Beauty

My pain wasn't always romantic like the poetry I write,
and it wasn't as beautiful as a Lana del Ray song.
My pain was messy, bloody, and aggravating,
but not as artistic as the female rage you see in movies.
My path of healing wasn't inspiring or cleansing like a fresh shower,
instead, it was suffocating darkness at 3 A.M.
My past didn't make me strong like the heroine in stories,
but tore me apart leaving only a stranger in the mirror
who had to pretend everything was okay
like an actor in a low-budget film.
My story isn't a story where I eventually blossomed into a fiery flower
or became the monster everyone feared,
instead, I am just a writer who is fueled by anger and spite.

<u>Fairy Tale Wishes</u>

I wish I could've saved you from many things in this life,
like from the girl who ruined your trust,
from the rotten arguments with your sister,
from the hesitating thoughts
and doubts in your head,
from your adrenaline rush addiction,
I wish I could've saved you from the world,
from yourself.
As those pretty eyes and soul
don't deserve anything less than peace,
and I wish you could've saved me too
but that kind of thing only happens in fairy tales.

-Happy endings aren't real

<u>Almost 20</u>

August 1st,
nearing the end of the year.
It only feels like it's just begun,
but I've been 19 for 9 months.
I'm not ready to move on,
And yet, it seems the year
begins to move faster and faster.

-I'm not ready to go yet

<u>Hide And Seek</u>

I promise I tried to hide it,
I tried to hide from it,
masking it with a smile
and snarky comment,
but somehow it found me
in that quiet hotel,
near run-down elevators,
it found me,
and I didn't have to put up much of a fight
for it to tear me apart this time.

<u>Isolation Or Depression</u>

Isolation is a funny thing,
as I will spend hours a day alone,
comfortable in my own silence,
but as soon as I lay my head down to rest,
wrapping myself in cool sheets,
constantly tossing and turning
in desperate search of warmth.
tears begin to rush from my eyes.
and in that moment,
I have never felt so alone.

The Immoral And Relentless

When the world finally tires of my being,
and I am laid to rest eternally,
know that my soul will remain among the living,
in the form of my work which I have bled myself dry for,
and each soul who reads of my love and misery,
will forever be haunted by my unruly spirit,
and as I welcome death like a forgotten memory,
I shall leave the restless piece of my soul behind,
to those who seek its companionship,
for I hope its' fire ignites their own soul as it once did mine.

-I hope my death means something

About The Author

Written at 19, in the middle of a deployment for the Texas Army National Guard and published at 20 while nearly 6 months pregnant. I, Nicole Music Hernandez, thank you for taking the time to read my first book that I have spent countless hours working to self-publish.

If you'd like to see more of me and updates about my future books, check me out on Instagram @n_hernandez_212

www.ingramcontent.com/pod-product-compliance
Lightning Source LLC
Chambersburg PA
CBHW070512160726
48003CB00004B/1536